The Senate

The Senate

Donald A. Ritchie

CHELSEA HOUSE PUBLISHERS

Editor-in-Chief: Nancy Toff
Executive Editor: Remmel T. Nunn
Managing Editor: Karyn Gullen Browne
Copy Chief: Juliann Barbato
Picture Editor: Adrian G. Allen
Art Director: Giannella Garrett
Manufacturing Manager: Gerald Levine

Staff for THE SENATE

Senior Editor: Elizabeth L. Mauro
Associate Editor: Pierre Hauser
Assistant Editor: Michele A. Merens
Copyeditor: Terrance Dolan
Editorial Assistant: Tara P. Deal
Picture Researcher: Sara Day
Designer: Noreen M. Lamb
Production Coordinator: Joseph Romano

Creative Director: Harold Steinberg

3   5   7   9   8   6   4   2

Library of Congress Cataloging in Publication Data

Ritchie, Donald A., 1945–
   The Senate.
   (Know your government)
   Bibliography: p.
   Includes index.
   Summary: Surveys the history of the Senate, with descriptions of its structure, current function, and influence on American society.
   1. United States. Congress. Senate—Juvenile literature. [1. United States. Congress. Senate] I. Title. II. Series: Know your government (New York, N.Y.)
JK1276.R57   1988   328.73′071   87-23840
ISBN 1-55546-121-2
      0-7910-0873-8 (pbk.)

CONTENTS

KNOW YOUR GOVERNMENT

CHELSEA HOUSE PUBLISHERS

INTRODUCTION

Government: Crises of Confidence

Arthur M. Schlesinger, jr.

From the start, Americans have regarded their government with a mixture of reliance and mistrust. The men who founded the republic did not doubt the indispensability of government. "If men were angels," observed the 51st Federalist Paper, "no government would be necessary." But men are not angels. Because human beings are subject to wicked as well as to noble impulses, government was deemed essential to assure freedom and order.

At the same time, the American revolutionaries knew that government could also become a source of injury and oppression. The men who gathered in Philadelphia in 1787 to write the Constitution therefore had two purposes in mind. They wanted to establish a strong central authority and to limit that central authority's capacity to abuse its power.

To prevent the abuse of power, the Founding Fathers wrote two basic principles into the new Constitution. The principle of federalism divided power between the state governments and the central authority. The principle of the separation of powers subdivided the central authority itself into three branches—the executive, the legislative, and the judiciary—so that "each may be a check on the other." The *Know Your Government* series focuses on the major executive departments and agencies in these branches of the federal government.

The Constitution did not plan the executive branch in any detail. After vesting the executive power in the president, it assumed the existence of "executive departments" without specifying what these departments should be. Congress began defining their functions in 1789 by creating the Departments of State, Treasury, and War. The secretaries in charge of these departments made up President Washington's first cabinet. Congress also provided for a legal officer, and President Washington soon invited the attorney general, as he was called, to attend cabinet meetings. As need required, Congress created more executive departments.

Setting up the cabinet was only the first step in organizing the American state. With almost no guidance from the Constitution, President Washington, seconded by Alexander Hamilton, his brilliant secretary of the treasury, equipped the infant republic with a working administrative structure. The Federalists believed in both executive energy and executive accountability and set high standards for public appointments. The Jeffersonian opposition had less faith in strong government and preferred local government to the central authority. But when Jefferson himself became president in 1801, although he set out to change the direction of policy, he found no reason to alter the framework the Federalists had erected.

By 1801 there were about 3,000 federal civilian employees in a nation of a little more than 5 million people. Growth in territory and population steadily enlarged national responsibilities. Thirty years later, when Jackson was president, there were more than 11,000 government workers in a nation of 13 million. The federal establishment was increasing at a faster rate than the population.

Jackson's presidency brought significant changes in the federal service. He believed that the executive branch contained too many officials who saw their jobs as "species of property" and as "a means of promoting individual interest." Against the idea of a permanent service based on life tenure, Jackson argued for the periodic redistribution of federal offices, contending that this was the democratic way and that official duties could be made "so plain and simple that men of intelligence may readily qualify themselves for their performance." He called this policy rotation-in-office. His opponents called it the spoils system.

In fact, partisan legend exaggerated the extent of Jackson's removals. More than 80 percent of federal officeholders retained their jobs. Jackson discharged no larger a proportion of government workers than Jefferson had done a generation earlier. But the rise in these years of mass political parties gave federal patronage new importance as a means of building the party and of rewarding activists. Jackson's successors were less restrained in the distribu-

8

tion of spoils. As the federal establishment grew—to nearly 40,000 by 1861—the politicization of the public service excited increasing concern.

After the Civil War the spoils system became a major political issue. High-minded men condemned it as the root of all political evil. The spoilsmen, said the British commentator James Bryce, "have distorted and depraved the mechanism of politics." Patronage, by giving jobs to unqualified, incompetent, and dishonest persons, lowered the standards of public service and nourished corrupt political machines. Office-seekers pursued presidents and cabinet secretaries without mercy. "Patronage," said Ulysses S. Grant after his presidency, "is the bane of the presidential office." "Every time I appoint someone to office," said another political leader, "I make a hundred enemies and one ingrate." George William Curtis, the president of the National Civil Service Reform League, summed up the indictment. He said,

> The theory which perverts public trusts into party spoils, making public
> employment dependent upon personal favor and not on proved merit,
> necessarily ruins the self-respect of public employees, destroys the
> function of party in a republic, prostitutes elections into a desperate
> strife for personal profit, and degrades the national character by lower-
> ing the moral tone and standard of the country.

The object of civil service reform was to promote efficiency and honesty in the public service and to bring about the ethical regeneration of public life. Over bitter opposition from politicians, the reformers in 1883 passed the Pendleton Act, establishing a bipartisan Civil Service Commission, competitive examinations, and appointment on merit. The Pendleton Act also gave the president authority to extend by executive order the number of "classified" jobs—that is, jobs subject to the merit system. The act applied initially only to about 14,000 of the more than 100,000 federal positions. But by the end of the 19th century 40 percent of federal jobs had moved into the classified category.

Civil service reform was in part a response to the growing complexity of American life. As society grew more organized and problems more technical, official duties were no longer so plain and simple that any person of intelligence could perform them. In public service, as in other areas, the all-round man was yielding ground to the expert, the amateur to the professional. The excesses of the spoils system thus provoked the counter-ideal of scientific public administration, separate from politics and, as far as possible, insulated against it.

The cult of the expert, however, had its own excesses. The idea that administration could be divorced from policy was an illusion. And in the realm of policy, the expert, however much segregated from partisan politics, can

9

never attain perfect objectivity. He remains the prisoner of his own set of values. It is these values rather than technical expertise that determine fundamental judgments of public policy. To turn over such judgments to experts, moreover, would be to abandon democracy itself; for in a democracy final decisions must be made by the people and their elected representatives. "The business of the expert," the British political scientist Harold Laski rightly said, "is to be on tap and not on top."

Politics, however, were deeply ingrained in American folkways. This meant intermittent tension between the presidential government, elected every four years by the people, and the permanent government, which saw presidents come and go while it went on forever. Sometimes the permanent government knew better than its political masters; sometimes it opposed or sabotaged valuable new initiatives. In the end a strong president with effective cabinet secretaries could make the permanent government responsive to presidential purpose, but it was often an exasperating struggle.

The struggle within the executive branch was less important, however, than the growing impatience with bureaucracy in society as a whole. The 20th century saw a considerable expansion of the federal establishment. The Great Depression and the New Deal led the national government to take on a variety of new responsibilities. The New Deal extended the federal regulatory apparatus. By 1940, in a nation of 130 million people, the number of federal workers for the first time passed the 1 million mark. The Second World War brought federal civilian employment to 3.8 million in 1945. With peace, the federal establishment declined to around 2 million by 1950. Then growth resumed, reaching 2.8 million by the 1980s.

The New Deal years saw rising criticism of "big government" and "bureaucracy." Businessmen resented federal regulation. Conservatives worried about the impact of paternalistic government on individual self-reliance, on community responsibility, and on economic and personal freedom. The nation in effect renewed the old debate between Hamilton and Jefferson in the early republic, although with an ironic exchange of positions. For the Hamiltonian constituency, the "rich and well-born," once the advocate of affirmative government, now condemned government intervention, while the Jeffersonian constituency, the plain people, once the advocate of a weak central government and of states' rights, now favored government intervention.

In the 1980s, with the presidency of Ronald Reagan, the debate has burst out with unusual intensity. According to conservatives, government intervention abridges liberty, stifles enterprise, and is inefficient, wasteful, and arbitrary. It disturbs the harmony of the self-adjusting market and creates worse troubles than it solves. Get government off our backs, according to the popular cliché, and our problems will solve themselves. When government is necessary, let it be at the local level, close to the people. Above all, stop the inexorable growth of the federal government.

In fact, for all the talk about the "swollen" and "bloated" bureaucracy, the federal establishment has not been growing as inexorably as many Americans seem to believe. In 1949, it consisted of 2.1 million people. Thirty years later, while the country had grown by 70 million, the federal force had grown only by 750,000. Federal workers were a smaller percentage of the population in 1985 than they were in 1955—or in 1940. The federal establishment, in short, has not kept pace with population growth. Moreover, national defense and the postal service account for 60 percent of federal employment.

Why then the widespread idea about the remorseless growth of government? It is partly because in the 1960s the national government assumed new and intrusive functions: affirmative action in civil rights, environmental protection, safety and health in the workplace, community organization, legal aid to the poor. Although this enlargement of the federal regulatory role was accompanied by marked growth in the size of government on all levels, the expansion has taken place primarily in state and local government. Whereas the federal force increased by only 27 percent in the 30 years after 1950, the state and local government force increased by an astonishing 212 percent.

Despite the statistics, the conviction flourishes in some minds that the national government is a steadily growing behemoth swallowing up the liberties of the people. The foes of Washington prefer local government, feeling it is closer to the people and therefore allegedly more responsive to popular needs. Obviously there is a great deal to be said for settling local questions locally. But local government is characteristically the government of the locally powerful. Historically, the way the locally powerless have won their human and constitutional rights has often been through appeal to the national government. The national government has vindicated racial justice against local bigotry, defended the Bill of Rights against local vigilantism, and protected natural resources against local greed. It has civilized industry and secured the rights of labor organizations. Had the states' rights creed prevailed, there would perhaps still be slavery in the United States.

The national authority, far from diminishing the individual, has given most Americans more personal dignity and liberty than ever before. The individual freedoms destroyed by the increase in national authority have been in the main the freedom to deny black Americans their rights as citizens; the freedom to put small children to work in mills and immigrants in sweatshops; the freedom to pay starvation wages, require barbarous working hours, and permit squalid working conditions; the freedom to deceive in the sale of goods and securities; the freedom to pollute the environment—all freedoms that, one supposes, a civilized nation can readily do without.

"Statements are made," said President John F. Kennedy in 1963, "labelling the Federal Government an outsider, an intruder, an adversary. . . . The United States Government is not a stranger or not an enemy. It is the people of fifty states joining in a national effort. . . . Only a great national effort by a great people working together can explore the mysteries of space, harvest the products at the bottom of the ocean, and mobilize the human, natural, and material resources of our lands."

So an old debate continues. However, Americans are of two minds. When pollsters ask large, spacious questions—Do you think government has become too involved in your lives? Do you think government should stop regulating business?—a sizable majority opposes big government. But when asked specific questions about the practical work of government—Do you favor social security? unemployment compensation? Medicare? health and safety standards in factories? environmental protection? government guarantee of jobs for everyone seeking employment? price and wage controls when inflation threatens?—a sizable majority approves of intervention.

In general, Americans do not want less government. What they want is more efficient government. They want government to do a better job. For a time in the 1970s, with Vietnam and Watergate, Americans lost confidence in the national government. In 1964, more than three-quarters of those polled had thought the national government could be trusted to do right most of the time. By 1980 only one-quarter was prepared to offer such trust. But by 1984 trust in the federal government to manage national affairs had climbed back to 45 percent.

Bureaucracy is a term of abuse. But it is impossible to run any large organization, whether public or private, without a bureaucracy's division of labor and hierarchy of authority. And we live in a world of large organizations. Without bureaucracy modern society would collapse. The problem is not to abolish bureaucracy, but to make it flexible, efficient, and capable of innovation.

Two hundred years after the drafting of the Constitution, Americans still regard government with a mixture of reliance and mistrust—a good combination. Mistrust is the best way to keep government reliable. Informed criticism is the means of correcting governmental inefficiency, incompetence, and arbitrariness; that is, of best enabling government to play its essential role. For without government, we cannot attain the goals of the Founding Fathers. Without an understanding of government, we cannot have the informed criticism that makes government do the job right. It is the duty of every American citizen to know our government—which is what this series is all about.

Visitors gather in the Capitol's rotunda to tour the Senate. Interested tourists may visit senators' offices, attend committee hearings, or sit in the Senate galleries.

ONE

The Upper House

Many visitors to the Capitol enter its public galleries expecting to see a crowd of senators engaged in debate. Conditioned by movie and textbook images of the legislature, they envision dramatic arguments and stirring speeches. But such scenes are rare. Except during roll-call votes, in which all senators participate by answering "aye" or "nay" when their name is called, few senators can be found on the Senate floor. Instead, U.S. senators usually spend most of their working day in the offices, corridors, conference rooms, and committee chambers of the Capitol and nearby office buildings. There they hear testimony, conduct investigations, and quiz presidential nominees for executive and judicial posts. They meet with lobbyists, the press, and the public. They convene to build support for favorite measures, arrange compromises, and count heads to estimate their opposition. And they work with their staffs to develop much of the legislation that governs the nation.

When the framers of the Constitution created the Senate, they never anticipated that it would become such a busy and powerful institution. Wary of granting too much power to one governmental body, they divided legislative duties between the Senate and the House of Representatives. They intended for the House to originate and debate most legislation and for the smaller Senate to amend and perfect House bills. As outlined by the framers, the

Senate's primary duties were to advise the president and to approve treaties and nominations.

Nevertheless, the Senate has established itself as Congress's powerful upper house. As the nation has grown, the Senate and its powers have expanded and changed. When the first Senate convened in 1789, its elite members—chosen by state legislatures—met in secret. Today, popularly elected senators conduct business in televised sessions. And the business they conduct is no longer primarily advisory. The modern Senate fully involves itself in originating and debating legislation and exercises considerable influence over American foreign policy. Accordingly, the American people, who once largely ignored the Senate, today demand much from it. They require their senators to take a stand on the most controversial issues of the day. They also hold senators accountable for their actions. Constituents send mountains of mail, make thousands of telephone calls, and sometimes even travel to Capitol Hill to make their views known to their senators.

Many factors have influenced the Senate's development. Powerful senators—such as Daniel Webster, John Calhoun, and Henry Clay, who dominated the Senate during the 19th century—have captured the public imagination.

The Senate Foreign Relations Committee debates an issue during a televised session in the 1970s. In 1789, by contrast, the first Senate met in secret.

16

The Senate chamber as it appeared in the late 1800s. Antique furnishings adorn the modern Senate chamber and remind senators of their heritage.

Strong Senate majority leaders—such as Lyndon B. Johnson, who led the Senate Democrats during much of the 1950s—have increased the Senate's influence. Compelling events during the 1960s and 1970s—such as the Vietnam War and the Watergate scandal—have led the Senate to reassert its authority. Throughout the Senate's history, the ambiguity of the Constitution's guidelines has allowed the Senate to shape its powers in response to the nation's demands.

Modern senators still cherish many of the traditions handed down to them over the last 200 years. The Senate chamber, adorned with snuffboxes, spittoons, and antique furnishings, constantly reminds them of their heritage. Yet they realize that a democratic legislature must stand ready to adapt itself to the needs of the people.

The Senate's dynamic nature makes it one of the most exciting bodies in the national government. As one senator observed: "The heat of controversy, the force of public pressure, the spur of criticism, the stimulation of clashing opinions in the Senate and at home make a senator's job more difficult, but at the same time they release the last drop of adrenaline and add to the zest of living."

Thomas Jefferson, Alexander Hamilton, and George Washington (left to right) appear in this mural in the Senate Reception Room, located in the Capitol.

TWO

Origins of the Senate

From the beginning of the American Revolution in 1776 until the ratification of the Constitution in 1789, a unicameral (single-chamber) Congress constituted the entire federal government. Although it acted as the nation's highest authority, this Congress did not have the power to regulate commerce or levy taxes. Under the Articles of Confederation—the nation's first charter—those powers were vested in the states.

Concerned by this system's weaknesses, the nation's leaders decided to restructure the federal government. In the summer of 1787, they convened in Philadelphia to create a new national charter. This meeting, the Constitutional Convention, gave birth to the U. S. Senate.

During the convention, a debate raged between delegations from large states and those from smaller states. Large states proposed that the Constitution base congressional representation on population. Small states—fearing Congress would ignore their needs if large states had more congressmen—demanded that the Constitution grant each state an equal number of representatives. The demands seemed so far apart that convention chairman George Washington feared the entire meeting would fail.

But Washington's fears were unfounded. In July 1787, the delegates reached a compromise. Using the British Parliament's House of Commons and House of Lords as models, they created a bicameral (two-chamber) Congress. This new legislature contained a House of Representatives, with membership based

19

George Washington presides over the Constitutional Convention in 1787. The Constitution modified the existing government by creating a bicameral (two-chamber) Congress.

on states' populations, and a Senate, with two senators from each state, regardless of its size.

The Constitution's framers borrowed the title *Senate* from ancient Rome, where it meant "an assembly of old men." Indeed, the Roman Senate had been a council of elder aristocrats who served for life. Some delegates held similar ideas for the U.S. Senate. They proposed that senators be elected for life and serve without pay. But other delegates pointed out that this system would allow only the rich to serve. They also worried that Americans would reject a plan that so closely resembled the British system they had rebelled against.

For two months, the delegates debated this issue, along with other questions about the federal government. On September 17, 1787, they signed the final draft of the U.S. Constitution. Article I outlined Congress's powers, duties, and privileges.

The Constitutional Senate

Many of the provisions outlined in Article I apply to both houses of Congress. Section 3, however, specifically details the Senate's responsibilities. It established most of the rules that govern the modern Senate. In 200 years, only two amendments—the Seventeenth and the Twentieth—have altered these Constitutional guidelines.

Section 3 states that two senators from each state will be chosen by their state legislatures. (The Seventeenth Amendment later altered this procedure, providing for popular election of senators.) It also dictates that a senator's term will last six years. Furthermore, Section 3 staggers the election of senators; it states that the electorate will choose only one-third of the Senate every two years. This provision ensures continuity and reduces drastic political shifts that could affect the Senate's agenda.

Next, the Constitution requires a senator to have been a citizen of the United States for at least nine years and to be a resident of the state from which he is elected. Finally, senators must be at least 30 years old before they can take office (representatives must be at least 25). The framers added this clause to ensure that older, more experienced legislators serve in the upper house.

Section 3 also outlines the Senate's leadership. The vice-president of the United States presides over the Senate as its president. The president of the Senate cannot vote except to break a tie, and he cannot address the Senate without its permission. Nevertheless, he presides over the various proceed-

Senator Jacob Javits (left) on the campaign trail during the 1970s. The Seventeenth Amendment provides for popular election of senators.

21

ings, convening and adjourning sessions and directing activity on the Senate floor. In his absence, the president pro tempore, or pro tem (temporary), presides. The president pro tem is usually the most senior member of the majority party. The Senate has the right to choose the president pro tem and its other leaders, including committee chairs and the majority leader.

The Constitution grants the House of Representatives the right to impeach (formally charge) public officials for wrongdoing. But it accords the Senate the power to hear all impeachment cases, including those against a U.S. president. (If the president is tried, the chief justice of the United States must preside.) The Senate can convict an impeached official if a two-thirds majority votes for conviction. An impeachment conviction is not a criminal conviction, and such a judgment may not extend further than to remove a person from office and disqualify him or her from holding other offices or titles. The judiciary may later indict, try, convict, and imprison the offender.

Other parts of the Constitution, though they are not exclusively related to the Senate, also define its powers. Article II gives the Senate sole authority to confirm presidential nominations and to ratify treaties. Article I, Section 7 outlines the procedures for initiating, passing, and enacting bills, and grants both houses the power to originate any legislation except revenue bills. (The House reserves the sole right to create revenue bills, although the Senate can

Vice-president Harry S. Truman (standing) presides over the Senate in 1945. In the vice-president's absence, the president pro tempore presides over the Senate.

22

President William Howard Taft signs bills granting statehood to New Mexico and Arizona in 1912. After a bill is passed by Congress, it goes to the president for approval or veto.

amend them.) Section 7 also states that after both houses pass a bill, they must send it to the president for approval or veto. If the president approves and signs the bill, it becomes law. If the president vetoes the bill, the Senate and the House must vote by a two-thirds majority to override the veto.

Under Article I, Section 8 the Senate and the House share equal jurisdiction over many issues: declaring war, maintaining armed forces, collecting taxes, borrowing money, minting currency, regulating commerce, establishing post offices, and making "all laws which shall be necessary and proper for carrying into execution the . . . powers vested by this Constitution." The Constitution grants both houses control over their own elections, rules, and internal procedures. It also requires each house to keep and publish a journal of its proceedings.

Although the Senate's powers have grown and developed over the years, it still plays the role that the Constitution's framers intended. The story goes that when Thomas Jefferson returned from France, where he had been serving as ambassador at the time the Constitution was being written, he asked George Washington why a Senate was necessary. Washington responded: "Why did you pour that coffee into the saucer?" "To cool it," Jefferson answered. "Even so," said Washington, "we pour legislation into the senatorial saucer to cool it."

In this 1789 painting, Vice-president John Adams gazes out the window of the Senate chamber in New York City's Federal Hall. Adams presided over the Senate's historic first session.

THREE

The Growth of
Power

At sunrise on March 4, 1789, church bells pealed in New York City—then the nation's capital—to honor the new federal government. But Senate business did not begin immediately. Before it could start, enough senators had to reach New York to establish a quorum—the minimum number of members needed to conduct business. Finally, on April 6, 1789, the first U.S. Senate convened, with 12 of its 22 senators in attendance. Vice-president John Adams presided.

The First Senate

The first Senate immediately got down to business. It established three Cabinet departments—War, State, and Treasury; created the federal judiciary; and passed the first ten amendments to the Constitution that form the Bill of Rights.

Recognizing the need for effective communication between the houses of Congress, the first Senate helped devise a method for delivering messages to and from the House. (Each house assigned a clerk to carry the messages.) Unwillingly, the original members also established equal pay for senators and representatives. The senators had originally voted salaries of seven dollars per day for themselves and six dollars per day for representatives. But the House objected and the Senate conceded the issue.

In August 1789, President Washington traveled to the Senate chamber to seek advice concerning Indian treaties. Some senators felt uncomfortable debating in Washington's presence, however, and they stalled the proceedings. The Senate did eventually offer its advice, but Washington never again attempted to participate in Senate deliberations. This tradition has endured. Subsequent presidents have never appeared in the Senate chamber when members are debating issues.

Some of the first Senate's traditions did not endure. For example, the first senators debated in private, whereas the House held open sessions. Naturally, newspapers devoted more attention to the House's lively, public debates than to the secretive meetings of the Senate. The public began clamoring for an open Senate. In 1794, the Senate yielded to public pressure and opened its doors for all legislative business. (Meetings to discuss executive matters, such as debates over treaties and nominations, remained closed until 1929.)

Politics and the Senate

When the first Senate met, organized political parties had not yet been formed. But sharply different opinions divided senators who wanted a strong federal

In 1806, New Hampshire senator William Plumer complained about the Senate's informal nature. The senators of that time were the youngest in the nation's history.

During the presidency of James Madison some senators refused to seek reelection and others resigned their seats in midterm because they found the Senate to be too quiet.

government from those who favored states' rights (granting states the power to direct all affairs within their borders). Senators who favored a national bank, protective trade tariffs (taxes on imported goods), and other vestiges of a strong federal government grouped together into the Federalist party. Their opposition became known as the Democratic-Republicans.

For the Senate's first 11 years, the Federalists enjoyed a majority. Steadily, however, the Democratic-Republicans gained strength. In 1800, the same year that the nation moved its capital to Washington, D.C., the Democratic-Republicans won their first Senate majority. Their leader, Thomas Jefferson, won the presidency.

The Jeffersonian Senate was the youngest in the nation's history. The average age of its senators was 40. In 1806, New Hampshire senator William Plumer described the informal nature of the young Senate. "[M]any of those that are there, are either writing letters or reading newspapers," he complained. "At the fireside a majority is seated, and often in a private conversation the question under debate is there settled by a free interchange of opinions."

The young, informal Senate was also restless. During the presidencies of Jefferson and his successor, James Madison, some senators refused to seek reelection. Others resigned their seats in midterm. Many simply found the Senate to be too quiet. When Henry Clay resigned his Senate seat to run for the House in 1811 (he later returned to the Senate), he said he preferred "the turbulence (if I may be allowed the term) of a numerous body to the solemn stillness of the Senate Chamber."

War and the Senate

The Senate faced other problems during Madison's presidency. Great Britain and France were at war, and Britain began to confiscate American ships that were trading with France. Furthermore, the British seized American seamen from merchant ships and "impressed" (forced) them into the British navy. Congressional "war hawks," mostly from western states, demanded that the

The Capitol lies in ruins after being burned by British troops in August 1814. Congressional business proceeded in temporary quarters until the Capitol was rebuilt in 1819.

nation defend its maritime rights. Moderate senators, mostly from New England, opposed war. Madison sided with the war hawks. At his request, the Senate declared war against Britain on June 18, 1812.

Many people expected the United States to win the War of 1812 easily. But in August 1814, British troops stormed Washington, D.C., and burned the Capitol building. Fearing that the government would move elsewhere, concerned Washington citizens erected a temporary site. The makeshift headquarters enabled congressional business to proceed, and the government stayed in Washington. Meanwhile, work to rebuild the Capitol began.

Standing Committees in the Senate

After the United States won the war in 1815, the Senate began to examine its legislative methods. It had always considered legislation in temporary committees. When an issue arose, it selected a few senators to study it. Those selected ultimately decided how the Senate would handle the issue.

This method had its problems. Powerful senators were appointed to committee after committee, whereas lesser-known senators served on very few committees. As a result, a handful of senators was conducting most of the nation's legislative business—and making most of the legislative decisions.

Clearly, the Senate needed a more equitable system. So in December 1816 it created the first standing (permanent) committees. Composed of Senate experts in certain fields, these committees lasted for the duration of each Senate term. The permanence of committee membership ensured that powerful or popular senators would not serve on every important committee.

The Missouri Compromise

In 1819, the 16th Senate met in its newly rebuilt chamber, where it faced problems caused by the nation's westward expansion. As thousands of pioneers moved west of the Mississippi River, new territories began applying for statehood. An important question arose: Would these new states permit or prohibit slavery?

The 16th Senate—like the nation itself—was equally divided between southern states, which depended upon slave labor, and northern states, which did not. Neither side wanted the other to gain a majority. In 1819, a northern

William Maclay: Diarist of the First U.S. Senate

When the new federal government was formed in 1789, the Pennsylvania state legislature elected
William Maclay and Robert Morris
as its two first U.S. senators. The
private journal that Maclay kept during his Senate term offers a unique
glimpse at the First Congress.

For the First Congress, there
were no precedents. The Senate had
to debate every action, no matter
how minute. In the following journal
entry, Maclay recounts the Senate's
deliberation over how it should conduct itself during President George
Washington's inaugural ceremony.

Senator William Maclay

*April 30, 1789 This is a great, important day. Goddess of etiquette, assist me
while I describe it. . . . The Senate met. The vice-president rose in the most solemn
manner. This son of Adam seemed impressed with deeper gravity, yet what shall I
think of him? He often, in the midst of the most important airs—I believe when he
is at loss for expressions (and this he often is, wrapped up, I suppose in the
contemplation of his own importance)—suffers an unmeaning kind of vacant laugh
to escape him.*

*This was the case today, and really to me bore the air of ridiculing the farce he was
acting. "Gentlemen, I wish for the direction of the Senate. The president will, I
suppose address the Congress. How shall I behave? How shall we receive it? Shall
it be standing or sitting?"*

*Here followed a considerable deal of talk from him which I could make nothing
of. Mr. Lee [senator from Virginia] began with the House of Commons (as is usual
with him), then the House of Lords, then the King, and then back again. The result
of his information was, that the Lords sat and the Commons stood on the delivery
of the King's speech. Mr. Izard [senator from South Carolina] got up and told how
often he had been in the House of Parliament. He said a great deal of what he had
seen there. [He] made, however, this sagacious discovery, that the Commons stood
because they had no seats to sit on. . . . It was discovered after some time that the
King sat, too, and had his robes and crown on.*

*Mr. Adams got up again and said he had been very often indeed at the Parliament
on those occasions, but there always was such a crowd, and ladies along, that for
his part he could not say how it was. Mr. Carroll [senator from Maryland] got up
to declare that he thought it of no consequence how it was in Great Britain; they were
no rule to us, etc. But all at once, the Secretary, who had been out, whispered to the
Chair that the Clerk from the Representatives was at the door with a communication.
Gentlemen of the Senate, how shall he be received?*

senator made a motion that the Senate prohibit slavery in Missouri. For three weeks, a bitter debate raged. Southern senators defended slavery as a positive practice; northerners denounced it as a moral evil.

In May 1820, North and South reached a compromise. The senators agreed to admit Missouri as a slave state and Maine as a free state. Thus, the number of slave and free states remained equal. The two sides also established an imaginary line across the remaining western territory along the 36° 30' latitude and prohibited slavery north of it, except in Missouri. This agreement, the Missouri Compromise, prevented a conflict between North and South—for the time being.

The Senate's Golden Age

In the early 1800s, the Federalist party dissolved. For a time, the Democratic-Republicans—now called simply the Democrats—ruled the Senate alone. This period was known as the Era of Good Feelings, because politics did not divide the Senate. These compatible relations ended in 1828, however, when Andrew Jackson was elected president. Although Jackson was a Democrat, his presidency once again divided the Senate's members into parties. It also fueled the animosity between northern and southern senators.

During this divisive period, the Senate became the center of debate about the nation's future. One of its most famous debates occurred in January 1830, when South Carolina senator Robert Hayne condemned the federal government. He proposed that the Senate accept states' rights to nullify federal laws. (States' rights were often proclaimed by southern leaders defending slavery.)

Daniel Webster of Massachusetts responded. He lambasted Hayne and other states' rights advocates for "speak[ing] of the Union in terms of indifference or even of disparagement." Undaunted, Hayne reiterated the doctrine that states could nullify any federal laws they opposed.

The next day, anxious spectators filled every seat in the Senate galleries to hear Webster's reply to the nullification theory. The speech they heard made history. Webster predicted that the doctrine would lead to war between the states. He called for national patriotism, closing his speech with the famous words, "Liberty and Union, now and forever, one and inseparable." Webster's speech, though rousing, did not lessen the split between North and South. Another issue also divided the Senate along regional lines. It involved rechartering the Bank of the United States (a government-chartered bank that

This portrait of President Andrew Jackson by Thomas Sully hangs in the Capitol. Jackson's rejection of a central banking system divided the Senate into opposing factions during the 1830s.

accepted both federal and private accounts). Democratic senators from western and southern states believed that the bank granted privileges to northern customers at the expense of the growing western and southern states. In response to the sentiments of his fellow party members, President Jackson vetoed the Senate's resolution to recharter the bank.

Jackson's opposition to the bank united the Senate's most powerful members—Daniel Webster, Henry Clay, and John C. Calhoun. They felt that the bank encouraged industrial development. To fight the Jacksonian Democrats, these senators formed a new party, the Whigs. The new party soon gained a majority in the Senate and resolved to fight Jackson's veto.

Tensions peaked in 1834 when the Whig majority voted to censure (officially reprimand) Jackson for his bank policy. No president—before or since—has ever received the Senate's censure. Nevertheless, Jackson refused to rescind his veto. The bank lost its charter, and in 1837 the Democrats expunged the censure resolution from the Senate Journal.

In 1840 the Whigs won the presidency, as well as majorities in the Senate and House. Whig senators attempted to renew the bank issue. Clay urged President William Henry Harrison to call a special session of Congress to create a new federal bank and enact other Whig legislation.

Unfortunately for the Whigs, Harrison died only one month after his inauguration. The new president, John Tyler, favored more limited government. He killed many Whig bills, and the Whigs could not muster the necessary two-thirds majority to override the presidential vetoes. The bank bill died, and political divisions within the Senate increased.

In an 1830 debate, Senator Daniel Webster (standing) responds to Senator Robert Hayne's proposal that the Senate acknowledge the right of individual states to ignore federal laws.

An 1834 political cartoon depicts President Jackson as king, satirizing his extensive use of presidential veto power. To oppose Jackson, powerful senators formed the Whig party.

President John Tyler favored a limited federal government and vetoed many Whig bills. During his administration, political divisions within the Senate increased.

The Wilmot Proviso

In 1846, the United States entered a war with Mexico over Texas's boundaries. The Mexican War reawakened the slavery question and increased hostilities between North and South. At issue was the Wilmot Proviso, an amendment to a war negotiations bill. Presented before the House by Congressman David Wilmot of Pennsylvania, the bill proposed that Congress prohibit slavery in all Mexican territories settled by American pioneers.

The House, which had a majority of members from the populous North, approved the Wilmot Proviso. But the Senate, equally divided between slaveholding and free states, repeatedly defeated it. Senators formerly allied along party lines began to split into regional factions. Calhoun, a Whig from South Carolina, introduced resolutions declaring that the Constitution protected slavery. The resolutions failed to pass, and the slavery issue continued to divide Congress. House and Senate leaders searched frantically for a compromise to save the Union.

Many congressional leaders placed their hope in Senator Clay, "the Great Compromiser." Although Clay had previously retired from the Senate, he returned to propose an omnibus bill, a package of solutions that attempted to appease North and South alike. He proposed that Congress admit California to the Union as a free state and allow the settlers of the New Mexico territory to decide the slavery question for themselves. He also recommended that

Senator John C. Calhoun, a Whig from South Carolina, introduced resolutions in 1846 declaring that the Constitution protected slavery in the South. His resolutions failed to pass.

Retired senator Henry Clay returned to the Senate in 1846 to propose a compromise that attempted to appease northern and southern senators who disagreed about states' rights to allow slavery.

Congress end the slave trade in the District of Columbia and pass a more effective fugitive-slave law.

Clay delivered several emotional speeches in support of his bill. At one point, he held a fragment of Washington's coffin before the Senate and begged its members to hear the "warning voice, coming from the grave to the Congress now in session to beware, to pause, to reflect before they lend themselves to any purposes which shall destroy the Union."

Fellow Whigs Webster and Calhoun joined Clay in debate for the last time. But they were not united. The aged Calhoun, so ill that another senator had to read his remarks, opposed the compromise. He warned that the southern states would secede from the Union if the Senate denied them an equal right to new territories. Webster, on the other hand, delivered the most eloquent defense of the compromise. "I wish to speak today, not as a Massachusetts man, nor as a northern man, but as an American, and a member of the Senate

Drama on the Senate Floor

In 1850, heated debates over the issue of slavery rocked the Senate. Pittsburgh journalist Jane Swisshelm traveled to Washington, D.C., to cover the debates for Horace Greeley's *New York Tribune* and, in doing so, became the first woman reporter to sit in the Senate's press gallery. The following excerpt recounts one of the Senate's most dramatic moments, when an argument between Mississippi senator Henry Foote—who thought Congress should allow settlers of the New Mexico territory to decide whether to allow slavery within its borders—and Missouri senator Thomas Hart Benton—who opposed this plan—erupted into pandemonium on the Senate floor.

Jane Swisshelm

Mr. Greeley—If you only had been here to see! But no, there were too many here just as it was. Such a scene as our Senate Chamber did present an hour ago! Col. Benton and Gen. Foote made quite an exhibition, but it would be hard to tell whether it was a farce, a comedy or a spirited tragedy. . . . [Foote] started running up the narrow aisle toward the President's desk and looking back over his shoulder as he got a pistol out of his side pocket. . . . Glancing back, I saw Col. Benton in the passage that runs around under the gallery and behind the seats. . . . Some gentlemen in the passage thought Mr. Benton was leaving the Chamber in anger, but Lieut. Gov. Dickinson of your state says he knew from the manner in which he thrust his chair back, that he intended to attack Mr. Foote. . . . Some gentlemen took [Benton] back to his own place, and Mr. Foote was calling upon them to let him come on, he was prepared. Someone caught his arm and Mr. Dickinson took the weapon from him. . . . Just here was all confusion, the President's hammer going but scarcely heard, the men in the gallery swearing, the members on the floor rushing up and calling all manner of order and disorder. Mr. Foote was taken back to his seat, and Col. Benton now appeared to have learned that his antagonist was armed. . . . He appeared fairly insane with rage—was trying to get off his coat, and thundering, "Let me go!" to those who were holding him. . . . I thought Benton's clothes would have all been torn to ribbons. As many as could get hold of him clutched him tightly, while some moved desks and chairs to give room. . . . It was too comical, in the very midst of the scene, to see Dickinson stand up as cool as a cucumber, after he had locked up the pistol and call, loud enough to be heard above all, for "the business before the Senate—the amendment of the Hon. Senator from Missouri."

In this 1850 political cartoon, Senator Henry Foote, who supported Clay's compromise, aims a pistol at Senator Thomas Hart Benton, who opposed the compromise.

of the United States," he said. "I speak today for the preservation of the Union."

Emotions ran high during the debate. At one point, Senator Henry Foote of Mississippi, who favored the compromise, pulled a pistol on Senator Thomas Hart Benton of Missouri, who opposed the compromise. "Stand out of the way and let the assassin fire!" Benton shouted. Other senators pulled the two men apart. Clay's bill began to unravel as some senators moved to strip it of sections they opposed.

The debate took its toll on Clay, who spoke for the compromise some 70 times. He left Washington for a rest, and the bill's proponents asked young Stephen Douglas, chairman of the committee on territories, to lead their cause. Douglas reexamined the bill, section by section. He modified each section to pacify as many states as possible. By pulling different factions behind each section of the bill he won passage in only two weeks.

Despite the bill's passage, antislavery senator Salmon Chase warned that "the question of slavery in the territories has been avoided. It has not been settled." His warning rang true. Four years later the slavery issue exploded again. And ironically, Douglas lit the fuse.

The Kansas-Nebraska Act

For years, Douglas had advocated constructing a transcontinental railroad, preferably through his home state of Illinois. He recognized that to accomplish this, the Senate would have to organize the Kansas and Nebraska territories into states in order to determine who owned the land on which the railroad would be built. Southerners objected, fearing that admitting these territories as states would upset the balance between slave and free states. Therefore, Douglas proposed a bill to void the Missouri Compromise and allow the settlers in the Kansas and Nebraska territories to decide the issue themselves.

The bill's opponents—composed of Whigs and antislavery Democrats—saw the Kansas-Nebraska bill as a plot to spread slavery into northern territories. They banded together and formed a new party, the Republicans, to fight it. Nevertheless, Congress passed the Kansas-Nebraska Act in 1854. But the

Senator Stephen Douglas proposed a bill to allow settlers in Kansas and Nebraska to decide whether they would allow slavery. Congress passed the Kansas-Nebraska Act in 1854.

An 1856 political cartoon shows South Carolina congressman Preston Brooks attacking Massachusetts senator Charles Sumner for denouncing slavery in Kansas.

outcome was not what Douglas had expected. Although the new states were mostly free, slavery existed in some areas. As a result, pro- and antislavery settlers turned Kansas into a battlefield.

The violence overflowed onto the Senate floor. In 1856, South Carolina congressman Preston Brooks went into the Senate chamber to seek revenge against Massachusetts senator Charles Sumner for a speech known as the "Crime Against Kansas," in which Sumner had denounced slavery in Kansas, which he believed should be a free state. Brooks marched to Sumner's desk and violently beat the senator on the head with his cane. During Sumner's recuperation, his empty desk stood as a reminder of the hostility between North and South.

The Senate meets in its new chamber which was added to the Capitol in 1859 to reduce crowding as the Senate expanded to include senators from newly admitted states.

FOUR

A House Divided

In January 1859, the Senate met in its original Washington chamber for the last time. The addition of new states—and thus, new senators—had caused such overcrowding that a new Senate chamber had to be added to the Capitol. As the senators prepared to move, Senator John J. Crittenden took the floor. "This chamber has been the scene of great events," he said. "Here questions of American constitutions and laws have been decided, questions of war and peace have been debated and decided. . . . They give a sort of consecrated character to this Hall." Then the senators proceeded down the corridor to their large, new chamber.

The Senate had barely settled into its new quarters when antislavery Republican Abraham Lincoln won the 1860 presidential election. Lincoln's election spurred the southern states to secede from the Union. Mississippi senator Jefferson Davis delivered the southern senators' collective farewell to the Senate. "I but express their desire when I say I hope and they hope for peaceable relations with you, though we must part," he said. As spectators wept in the galleries, Davis slowly left the chamber. The other seceding senators followed.

The withdrawal of so many southern Democrats gave the young Republican party its first Senate majority. The remaining Democrats were so badly

Mississippi senator Jefferson Davis, photographed by Mathew Brady. After the southern states seceded from the Union in 1861, Davis delivered the southern senators' farewell to the Senate.

outnumbered that they did not bother to hold caucuses (closed meetings to decide policy) and frequently boycotted debates. As a result, many committee chairmanships shifted from southern, proslavery senators to northern, antislavery legislators.

After the Civil War began in April 1861, the Republican Senate focused on two goals: restoring the Union and enacting Republican domestic programs. On July 4, 1861, President Lincoln called the Senate into special session to request the funds and authority to raise Union military forces. The senators promptly approved his request, enacting the nation's first income tax, adding tariffs to previously duty-free items, and levying new taxes on alcohol and tobacco. They voted to draft able-bodied young men into the army. And they passed the Legal Tender Act, which allowed the government to print the nation's first paper currency, called "greenbacks."

President Abraham Lincoln, photographed at the height of the Civil War in 1863. While the war raged, Senate Republicans enacted laws that southern Senate Democrats had long opposed.

A "greenback," the nation's first paper currency. When the Senate passed the Legal Tender Act in 1861, it enabled the government to print paper money to pay for Union army needs.

Some senators became actively involved in the war. When fighting broke out at Bull Run, just 30 miles from the Capitol, many senators traveled to the battlefield to observe it. The senators fled with the Union troops after unexpected Confederate reinforcements arrived. Later in the war, Oregon senator Edward Baker died leading Union troops at the Battle of Ball's Bluff.

While the war raged, the Senate also attended to other business. In 1862, it enacted the Homestead Act, providing free land to farmers in the western territories. It passed legislation to promote construction of the first transcontinental railroad. And it passed the Morrill Land Grant Act, granting public lands to fund agricultural and mechanical colleges. This burst of legislative activity helped the Republicans establish programs that the Democrats had frustrated for decades. Senator Sumner commented that "Never. . . . since I have been in Congress has it come together in such tranquillity."

President Andrew Johnson favored lenient reconstruction policies for the South. He outraged Senate Republicans by vetoing bills that would have protected freedmen's rights.

The Senate was out of session when the Confederate army surrendered in April 1865. President Lincoln hoped to take advantage of the Senate's absence and enact his reconstruction program—a plan for rebuilding the South into a productive part of the Union. But his assassination later that month left reconstruction in the hands of his successor, Andrew Johnson.

Johnson had been a Democratic senator from Tennessee when the South seceded. He won favor with radical Republicans by refusing to secede with his state. The radicals now hoped that Johnson would support civil rights for freedmen. But they were disturbed by Johnson's lenient policies toward the South. And they were outraged when he vetoed the Freedmen's Bureau and civil rights bills, which would have protected freedmen's rights and helped their transition from slavery to freedom.

The radicals responded to these vetoes by enacting the Tenure of Office Act, a bill forbidding the president to replace federal officers without the Senate's consent. The act was intended to prevent Johnson from replacing Secretary of War Edwin M. Stanton, who supported reconstruction. When

Johnson disregarded the act and fired Stanton, the House voted to impeach him. The Senate sat as a court of impeachment, but failed by a single vote to convict Johnson. Many moderate Republican senators voted to acquit him because they disliked the liberal politics of Vice-president Benjamin Wade, who would have become president if Johnson had been convicted.

The Gilded Age

A series of politically weak presidents followed Johnson, who left office in 1869. As a result, strong senators assumed greater authority and the Senate entered its Gilded Age, during which it became the most powerful body in the federal government. Its power was so great that Senator Justin Morrill turned down a cabinet appointment, declaring there was "no office to which I could be

Senator Justin Morrill refused a cabinet position in 1870 because he preferred to remain in the Senate. At this time, the Senate was the most powerful body in the federal government.

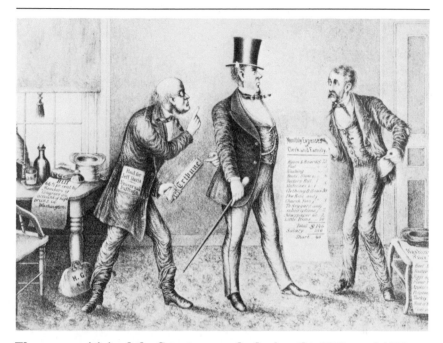

The press criticized the Senate severely during the 1870s and 1880s. This 1873 cartoon targets the "Salary Grab," a congressional attempt to raise senators' salaries.

appointed, that I would accept in preference to a seat in the United States Senate."

Despite the Senate's preeminence, the public and the press criticized it severely during the 1870s and 1880s. The public blamed the Senate's economic legislation for the financial panic of 1873 and the unsettled boom-and-bust period that followed. Newspapers accused congressmen of accepting stocks and money to pass legislation. And they lampooned a congressional attempt to raise salaries, calling it the "Salary Grab."

At the same time, corruption became the focus of intense public scrutiny. Some senators were powerful political bosses who used their seats to funnel federal patronage (government jobs and contracts) to their supporters. By the 1880s, civil service reformers were demanding changes in the inefficient and corrupt patronage system.

In response to these demands, President James Garfield challenged a patronage appointment made by New York senator Roscoe Conkling. After a

bitter fight, Conkling dramatically resigned from the Senate. But his resignation did not end the argument. On July 2, 1881, an office-seeker who had been denied patronage fatally shot Garfield.

The assassination stirred national sympathy for the civil service reform Garfield had supported. Senator George Pendleton of Ohio drafted a civil service act that called for eliminating political patronage and protecting federal employees from dismissal for political reasons. Congress passed the act in 1883.

Civil service reform did little to upset the balance of power in the Senate, however. Senatorial power continued to reside with the chairmen of the Senate's money committees—finance and appropriations. These chairmen became the Senate's most powerful members, serving as their respective parties' leaders in the Senate chamber. Senators who cooperated with them received choice assignments and legislative support. Those who advocated reform, on the other hand, received appointments to powerless committees. For example, committee chairmen appointed reformist senator Robert La Follette to the obscure Potomac Riverfront Committee. La Follette was given an isolated committee room—and no legislation to consider.

By the end of the 19th century, the press portrayed the Senate as a "Millionaire's Club" and described its committee chairmen as powerful legislative barons. The power commanded by committee chairmen stimulated muckraking newspaper and magazine articles, which alleged that senators promoted corporate welfare rather than the public good. Together with a rash of voting scandals, these attacks led to the ratification of the Seventeenth Amendment in 1913. The amendment established direct election of senators by

An 1881 cartoon satirizes Senator Roscoe Conkling's dramatic resignation from the Senate, after President Garfield challenged the senator's appointment of a supporter to a government job.

the people, instead of by state legislatures. From then on, any senator with hopes for reelection had to respond to his constituents' needs.

The Senate underwent a political revolution in the early 1900s, when the Republican ranks split between conservatives and progressives. This enabled Democrats to win their first Congressional majority in decades, in 1912. They used their new power to establish some Senate traditions. Democratic caucus chairman John Worth Kern of Indiana became the first to play the modern role of a strong party floor-leader. And J. Hamilton Lewis of Illinois became the Senate's first party whip—a member who enforces party discipline and secures attendance at important legislative sessions.

Also in 1912, Democrat Woodrow Wilson won the presidency. Wilson believed that Congress should function more like the British Parliament. He thought the president should personally manage the legislative process, as Britain's prime minister did. Therefore, he tried to work as chief legislator, actively promoting his legislative agenda.

Wisconsin senator Robert La Follette advocated civil service reform. Powerful Senate leaders who opposed his views attempted to limit his influence by appointing him to obscure Senate committees.

President Woodrow Wilson addresses Congress. Wilson believed he should personally manage the legislative process and actively promoted his legislative agenda.

Wilson scored repeated successes in domestic matters, but he suffered severe defeats in foreign policy. In 1919, the Senate rejected Wilson's proposal that America participate in the League of Nations, whose establishment he had negotiated at the end of World War I as part of the Treaty of Versailles. Wilson had hoped that the league would unite nations and help prevent another war. But many senators feared it would reduce America's ability to determine its own foreign policy, and the Senate defeated the treaty.

During the 1920s, conservative Republicans won majorities in both houses of Congress. Despite the continued efforts of progressive senators, such as Robert La Follette and George Norris, the newly conservative Senate turned

53

away from reform. Hoping to stimulate the economy, the Senate cut taxes for high incomes and raised tariffs to all-time highs. But economic conditions worsened and then suffered a monumental setback when the stock market crashed in 1929. The long depression that followed undermined the popularity of the Republicans' programs. In the 1932 elections, Democrats regained a Senate majority. And in the same year, Democrat Franklin D. Roosevelt defeated Republican incumbent Herbert Hoover for the presidency.

The New Deal

The new Democratic majority of the 73rd Congress lacked a clear agenda for ending the depression. But many felt that action—any action—was needed to

President Franklin D. Roosevelt (seated, second from right) with North Dakota farmers who received a 1936 drought relief grant. The Senate cooperated with Roosevelt to enact New Deal legislation.

In this 1936 cartoon, President Roosevelt confers with Congress about the health of the nation and offers a host of "New Deal remedies" to end the economic depression.

save the nation. So, during its first session, the 73rd Congress enacted a raft of legislation that composed Roosevelt's New Deal. The Senate was so eager to pass New Deal programs that some senators voted on legislation they had never read.

Members of the Senate proposed many New Deal measures. For example, Michigan senator Arthur H. Vandenberg promoted the Federal Deposit Insurance plan to protect individual bank accounts if banks failed. Louisiana senator Huey P. Long advocated a redistribution of the nation's wealth. And New York senator Robert Wagner formulated the Wagner Labor Act, which protected the right of unskilled laborers to organize into unions.

But the Senate did not always cooperate with Roosevelt. In 1937, for example, the president tried to appoint additional justices to the Supreme

55

Court, which had overturned some New Deal legislation. His opponents accused him of trying to "pack" the court, and a coalition of Democrats and Republicans in the Senate blocked the plan. Even after the Senate quashed the courtpacking plan, this coalition remained powerful. It later defeated Roosevelt's efforts to extend certain New Deal social programs.

World War II

Since the end of World War I the Senate had been dominated by isolationist senators, who were opposed to American involvement in foreign disputes. But in the late 1930s, as the war in Europe intensified, senators who thought the United States should intervene overseas won important votes. These votes

As chairman of the Senate Foreign Relations Committee in 1945, Senator Arthur Vandenberg supported such initiatives as the Marshall Plan for economic aid to Europe.

extended the military draft, suspended neutrality laws, and provided aid to the Allies fighting against Germany. When the Japanese attacked Pearl Harbor in December 1941, the Senate declared war. As a result of the war, many isolationists were defeated in their reelection bids.

The new public attitude toward foreign affairs affected many senators, including Vandenberg, one of the leading prewar isolationists. Near the war's end, he presented his famous "speech heard round the world," in which he claimed that the United States was no longer invulnerable to foreign attack. He pledged his support for "maximum American cooperation" with other nations to maintain peace in the postwar world.

After the war ended in 1945, Republican Vandenberg used his position as chairman of the Foreign Relations Committee to help the Democratic administration. He supported the Marshall Plan for economic aid to Europe; the Truman Doctrine protecting U.S. allies from Communist takeover; and the North Atlantic Treaty Organization, or NATO, a military alliance between the United States and Western Europe.

Although the committee supported these foreign-policy initiatives, the Republican-dominated 80th Congress strongly opposed most Democratic domestic programs. It did pass the Taft-Hartley Act (1947), which restricted labor-union activities. But it was unable to reverse the trend of federal expansion, and after two years, voters returned the Democrats to the majority.

The McCarthy Era

International issues occupied the Senate's immediate postwar years. In 1949, Communist forces came to power in China and soon signed a mutual friendship treaty with the Soviet Union. In 1950, Communist North Korea invaded South Korea. Some senators blamed these events on Communist subversion in the State Department and other agencies. In 1953, Senator Joseph R. McCarthy, chairman of the Government Operations Committee, began questioning hundreds of Americans about their alleged associations with the Communist party.

McCarthy interrogated writers, actors, statesmen, and scientists and even investigated government agencies. His infamous question, "Are you now, or have you ever been, a member of the Communist party?" sent chills throughout America's political and artistic communities. Often, McCarthy

Senator Joseph McCarthy (far right) with other members of the Government Operations Committee. In 1953, McCarthy began questioning hundreds of Americans about their alleged associations with the Communist party.

accused innocent people of being Communists. As a result of his investigation, scores of performers and others were blacklisted—denied work on the assumption that they were card-carrying Communists.

McCarthy's tactics stirred Margaret Chase Smith and a small group of other senators to issue a "Declaration of Conscience" against him. But the Senate tolerated him until his bullying during a televised hearing caused a public outcry. In December 1954, the Senate censured McCarthy for his abusive behavior.

Democratic Rule

In 1958, the Democrats won overwhelming majorities in both houses of Congress. Nevertheless, the Senate became a house divided, as conservatives and liberals battled for control. Conservative southern Democrats, who chaired most Senate committees, stalled enactment of liberal programs and civil rights bills. In response, liberal Democrats allied themselves with Republicans to pass civil rights legislation.

Senate majority leader Lyndon Johnson used his position to grant choice committee assignments to freshman Democrats who voted his way. He kept tight control on the Senate schedule, managing the major bills himself, rushing legislation through in batches by unanimous consent agreements, and holding very few party conferences (gatherings of Democratic senators to decide policies and strategies).

After Johnson became president in 1963, his legislative skills helped him build a supporting coalition in Congress. The coalition enacted his Great Society slate of social reforms, including Medicare for the aged, elementary and secondary school aid, other elements of his War on Poverty, and the Civil Rights Act of 1964, which outlawed racial discrimination in public accommodations, elections, and employment.

By 1967, however, disagreement over America's involvement in the Vietnam War—which began during the Eisenhower administration and escalated during the 1960s—had destroyed Johnson's coalition. Democrats who

Senator Margaret Chase Smith, shown here, rallied a small group of other senators to protest McCarthy's abusive investigation of Communist subversion during 1953 and 1954.

Lyndon B. Johnson on Senate Leadership

During most of Republican president Dwight D. Eisenhower's administration, Lyndon B. Johnson, a Democrat, served as Senate majority leader. From 1953 to 1960, Johnson led the Senate through one of its most powerful eras, paving the way for civil rights legislation and other social reforms in the next decade. In a 1960 interview with *U.S. News & World Report,* he shared some insights about Senate leadership.

On passing legislation

It's an 18-to-20-hour-a-day job. Each morning my staff puts on my desk the most important recommendations made by committees. They must be evaluated. And that's just the first step—studying the actual draftsmanship. The important thing is the feeling and the sectional interest and the national interest that went into a particular bill. A bill for roads may come to the floor and

Lyndon Johnson (center) joins hands with fellow senators shortly before his 1961 resignation from the Senate.

some Senator will say: "Now, wait a minute—that's not fair to the smaller states—and you've overlooked this point." Well, you had better not overlook it, because, if you do, your bill will be killed.

On leading the Senate

We do not have a dictatorship. The thing that most people do not understand is that the Majority Leader has no power, really, except the power of recognition [the opportunity to express viewpoints before any other Senator does]. . . . I sometimes think that the Senate has 98 leaders and two followers—that's Senator Dirksen [Senate minority leader] and I—we're the followers. We have to be guided by what these groups will support.

On the Senate's character

I think that most people want what you would call a "prudent progressivism." They want you to march forward, constantly going ahead, but never getting both feet off the ground at the same time. . . . I think the average member of the Senate accepts that philosophy, and I think that accounts for the unanimity with which the Senate has functioned. It debates a bill, and sometimes when you walk into the chamber you'd think that Senators were going to punch each others' eyes out, but the final result is a well-reasoned document. The President may not necessarily approve it, but it's amazing that he approves as many bills as he does, considering the divisions between us.

wanted to send more American aid and troops to anticommunist South Vietnam clashed with those who opposed continued American involvement in the war. And powerful senators, including majority leader Mike Mansfield and Foreign Relations Committee chairman J. William Fulbright, grew increasingly skeptical of the war's goals. Antiwar sentiment grew so strong that Johnson declined to run for reelection in 1968.

Nixon and the Senate

The Vietnam War continued under Johnson's successor, Richard Nixon. As a result, the Senate passed the War Powers Act. The act limited the president's authority to send troops into combat without congressional approval and expanded congressional authority to withdraw troops.

Nixon's clash with the Senate culminated in 1973, when the Senate began investigating the burglary of the Democratic national campaign headquarters at the Watergate office complex. The Senate created a special investigating

Onlookers watch as President Lyndon Johnson signs the Civil Rights Bill in 1968. The bill supplemented the Civil Rights Act of 1964, which outlawed racial discrimination in public accommodations, elections, and employment.

committee, chaired by Senator Sam Ervin of North Carolina, to determine if Nixon had been involved in the incident. The committee heard testimony and collected evidence that implicated Nixon in covering up the burglary. In August 1974, Nixon resigned to avoid impeachment.

Two presidents who immediately followed Nixon, Gerald Ford and Jimmy Carter, encountered considerable resistance in the Senate. Congress restricted their emergency powers, sought more control over the national budget and intelligence operations, rejected more than 100 presidential measures, and turned down many presidential nominees. Republican Ronald Reagan's election in 1980 carried a slim Republican majority into the Senate. Although the House remained Democratic, the Republicans made the most of this divided Congress and achieved remarkable party unity. Aided by Reagan's popularity, the

Demonstrators gather in Washington, D.C., to protest the Vietnam War in 1967. Powerful senators, including majority leader Mike Mansfield, also questioned U.S. involvement in the war.

Senators Howard Baker (left) and Sam Ervin (center) sit on the Senate's special investigating committee to determine President Richard Nixon's involvement in the Watergate scandal.

Republicans increased defense spending, instituted tax reform, and drastically cut the budgets of many social programs.

The modern Senate retains the Constitutional authority it received 200 years ago. But it has changed in size and character. The small, secretive body has become a powerful institution that strives, in the words of one senator, to reflect "the passion and conviction and ultimate common sense of the American people themselves."

The Capitol is one of the nation's supreme symbols of government. Here, and in nearby office buildings, senators work with their staffs to develop much of the legislation that governs the nation.

FIVE

The Modern Senate

Since the Senate's inception various structures have evolved to help ensure timely passage of legislation. Powerful majority and minority leaders organize their party's efforts and help steer bills through the Senate. Influential chairmen build support for bills, nominations, and treaties. And, almost unseen, staff members write, research, and otherwise support legislative efforts.

During the 20th century, the leader of the majority party has become the Senate's most important member. As Democratic leader Robert C. Byrd once explained, "The minority leader speaks for his party. But the majority leader, whether he be a Democrat or a Republican, is the leader of the Senate."

A majority leader's effectiveness depends on personality, political style, and circumstances. He needs a persuasive personality and a firm will to organize his ranks and bargain wisely. A leader also needs the political expertise to monitor committees, understand how the contents of bills are decided, and gauge the needs, problems, and personalities of individual senators. And a leader must know Senate rules well enough to steer bills through and to prevent the opposition from using shrewd parliamentary maneuvers to side-track legislation.

A minority leader needs skills similar to those of the majority leader. But his job differs somewhat because his party lacks the votes to carry a bill through the Senate. Majority leaders generally try to work with minority leaders in scheduling bills and votes. By consulting the minority leader in advance, the majority leader can achieve unanimous consent agreements that speed Senate business.

The Senate accords respect to both majority and minority leaders. By custom, the presiding officer always recognizes (calls upon) a majority or minority leader before recognizing other senators.

Party Whips

Party leaders greatly depend upon the assistance of their whips—senators elected to organize party business. The term *whip* comes from *whipper-in*, the

Senate majority and minority leaders (left to right) Alan Simpson, Robert Dole, Robert Byrd, and Alan Cranston meet in the Senate Reception Room in 1985.

person who keeps hounds from straying during a fox hunt. Whips ensure that senators are present when the Senate conducts important business. They send out weekly whip notices that senators can consult when planning their schedules.

When the Senate takes roll-call votes, whips announce the absence of any senators. To speed voting, they help arrange vote pairing, in which a senator agrees to cancel his vote by pairing it with an absent member who would have voted the opposite way. Whips also assist in head counting—polling senators in advance to determine which senators intend to vote for or against a bill and when enough votes have been secured to pass it.

Whips are elected because of their political abilities, their knowledge of the rules, and their talent for getting along with their colleagues. A whip's relationship with his party's leader has been compared to that between the president and vice-president. For example, whips stand in when their leaders are absent. Often, a party attempts to balance its leadership by choosing its whip and leader from different ideological wings of the party.

Committees and Their Chairmen

Much of the Senate's work is conducted in committees or subcommittees. Many different kinds of committee meetings crowd the Senate's daily schedule, and the public is allowed to attend most, except those that involve confidential matters. Standing (permanent) committees are established at the beginning of each Senate session and last for the entire term. They address issues that surface frequently, such as foreign relations and the budget. The 99th Congress (1985–1987) had 16 standing committees.

Select and special committees include committees on aging, ethics, Indian affairs, and national security. They meet to resolve issues as they arise. The Senate also participates in joint committees—panels composed of both senators and representatives. These include the joint committees on printing, taxation, and the Library of Congress.

Other committees are partisan (party) committees, which help develop programs, publish policy reports, and keep voting records. Party members appoint senators to these committees during party conferences. Party leaders serve on partisan committees and meet regularly with chairs of standing committees to keep track of legislation. Just as the majority leader schedules business on the Senate floor, committee chairs manage their committees' schedules. They attempt to build coalitions behind bills, nominations, and

A meeting of the Senate Foreign Relations Committee in 1978. Standing committees are established at the beginning of each session and meet for the entire term.

treaties. And, unless some other member of the committee has been especially identified with a bill, they also serve as floor managers, guiding bills through deliberations.

The Senate Staff

The Senate depends on a support staff of about 7,000 employees. Committee staffs may number 50 to 60 people each. The size of the staff in a senator's office depends upon the population of the state he or she represents. Staff members in Washington generate new legislative or investigative ideas, create reports, and write speeches. Other staff members work in their senator's home state, answering constituent requests and informing the senator of developments at home.

The Senate at large elects three staff members. The first, the secretary of the Senate, acts as its chief administrative officer. The secretary manages the Senate's internal finances, stationery supplies, and printed and archival documents. He supervises the parliamentarians who advise the presiding officer of the Senate's rules, and the clerks in the Senate chamber, the Senate Library, and the Historical Office. He also oversees the registration of lobbyists and campaign financial reports.

The second elected staff member, the sergeant at arms, is in charge of the doorkeepers, press galleries, pages, and the computer center, among other functions. Occasionally, when the Senate has been unable to establish a quorum, it has dispatched the sergeant at arms to summon senators to the chamber. The Senate chaplain, the third elected staffer, opens daily Senate sessions with a prayer and offers spiritual advice to senators and staff.

Another notable staff member is the Senate parliamentarian. Seated at the front desk in the chamber, the parliamentarian advises the presiding officer of the Senate's rules and precedents. The parliamentarian has frequently been called the "Senate's ventriloquist," because he whispers rules to the presiding officer, who then repeats them aloud.

The Senate prayer room is located in the Capitol. The vast Senate staff includes a chaplain, elected by the Senate at large.

Each party also elects staff members. The most notable is the party secretary. This staff member aids party leaders by counting heads for votes, maintaining the party cloakroom (a room near the Senate chamber where senators can meet), and keeping conference minutes.

Senate Headquarters

The Senate's center of operations has grown to meet its increased activities and size. The Capitol building, completed in the 1870s, has been joined by three Senate office buildings: the Richard Russell Building, completed in 1909; the Everett Dirksen Building, completed in 1958; and the Philip Hart Building, completed in 1982. Together, these three massive structures house the Senate's committees and staff members. A system of bells and lights within each building alerts senators to votes, quorum calls, and other legislative business. A network of tunnels and subways connects the Senate office buildings to the Capitol so senators can reach the chamber quickly if a vote is called.

Senate staff members conduct research in the Senate library. The secretary of the Senate oversees the management of the library.

A subway system connects Senate office buildings to the Capitol. Senators can take the subway to reach the chamber quickly when votes are called.

Most of the Capitol and the office buildings are open to the public. Citizens may visit senators' offices, attend committee hearings, or receive passes to sit in the Senate galleries and hear debates.

The Budget

Congressional appropriations fund Senate expenses. The Legislative Branch Subcommittee of the Senate Appropriations Committee recommends annual allocations for the Senate. Both the Senate and the House must vote on appropriations bills. Each senator receives staff and office expense funds based on the size of his state.

The Senate Rules and Administration Committee decides how Senate money can be spent and supervises additional expenses, such as Senate-related travel. The Senate financial clerk distributes all funds. Computers now handle the complex bookkeeping required to fund the Senate's greatly expanded operations.

For a bill to become law, the president must either sign it or fail to act on it within 10 days. Here, onlookers watch as President Harry Truman signs a bill into law.

SIX

How a Bill Becomes Law

The Senate spends most of each term considering proposed bills. Passing a bill is a complex affair that requires considerable work and resourcefulness. The process is so rigorous that Congress enacts only 5 percent of the approximately 20,000 bills introduced in each 2-year session.

Ideas for legislation come from numerous sources: the president, cabinet members, senators, staff members, lobbyists, organizations, and private citizens. If a senator becomes interested in an idea, he may sponsor a bill. At the sponsoring senator's request, staff members submit bill proposals to the office of the Senate's Legislative Counsel, which drafts the bill's language. The sponsoring senator may also request background research from such congressional support agencies as the Congressional Research Service, the General Accounting Office, the Congressional Budget Office, or the Office of Technology Assessment.

After the senator and his staff have researched the proposal and received a draft of the bill from the Legislative Counsel, the senator circulates the bill throughout the Senate. Other senators who support the bill may become its cosponsors. After cosponsors have been secured, the sponsoring senator rises at his desk in the Senate chamber and formally introduces the bill.

The legislative clerk assigns a number to every bill introduced. For example,

S.200 would represent the 200th bill introduced in a session. Senior senators reserve memorable bill numbers, such as S.1 and S.1776, to draw attention to special bills. After a number has been assigned, the parliamentarian refers the bill to the proper committee for consideration.

The Bill in Committee

Once in committee, the bill must compete with other measures for a place on the committee's agenda. Many bills die because they receive no committee attention. If the committee schedules the bill, it may assign it to a subcommittee—a portion of the committee with a specific area of jurisdiction.

After a Senate bill has been introduced by a sponsoring senator, it is assigned a number and referred to the proper committee for consideration.

II

100TH CONGRESS
1ST SESSION

S. 474

Making urgent supplemental appropriations for the fiscal year ending September 30, 1987, to support regional development programs of the Southern Africa Development Coordination Conference (SADCC).

IN THE SENATE OF THE UNITED STATES

FEBRUARY 4, 1987

Mr. KENNEDY (for himself, Mr. WEICKER, Mr. SPECTER, Mr. KERRY, Mr. SIMON, Mr. LEVIN, and Mr. BIDEN) introduced the following bill; which was read twice and referred to the Committee on Foreign Relations

---

A BILL

Making urgent supplemental appropriations for the fiscal year ending September 30, 1987, to support regional development programs of the Southern Africa Development Coordination Conference (SADCC).

1   *Be it enacted by the Senate and House of Representa-*
2   *tives of the United States of America in Congress assembled,*
3   **SECTION 1. SHORT TITLE.**
4   This Act may be cited as the "Urgent Supplemental
5   Appropriations For Southern Africa Act of 1987".
6   **SEC. 2. FINDINGS.**
7   The Congress makes the following findings:

74

A joint resolution is a formal opinion that has received approval from both the Senate and the House. It has the force of law when signed (or not acted on) by the president.

II

100TH CONGRESS
1ST SESSION
S. J. RES. 68

To designate March 11, 1987 as "National Operation Prom/Graduation Kickoff Day".

IN THE SENATE OF THE UNITED STATES

FEBRUARY 26, 1987

Mr. DECONCINI (for himself, Mr. HATCH, Mr. HOLLINGS, and Mr. BOSCHWITZ) introduced the following joint resolution; which was read twice and referred to the Committee on the Judiciary

---

JOINT RESOLUTION

To designate March 11, 1987 as "National Operation Prom/ Graduation Kickoff Day".

Whereas the Congress and the President have identified drug abuse as one of the greatest threats to the American Society;

Whereas the greatest threat of drug abuse is among our adolescent children;

Whereas thousands of young people die or are injured from drug or drugged driving and/or alcohol or drug abuse;

Whereas there is a great need for Federal, State, and local governments to become involved in educating our young Americans to the dangers associated with alcohol and drug abuse;

If the subcommittee takes up the bill, it may hold hearings in which expert witnesses, government officials, and concerned citizens testify about the bill's merits or deficiencies. Members of the presidential administration are frequently called to state the president's position on the bill. After the hearings end, the subcommittee votes on the measure.

If the subcommittee approves the measure, it sends the bill to the full committee. There, senators "mark up" the bill—reviewing its content, making revisions, and correcting its final wording. This process can be painfully slow. Senators may ignore the bill in favor of more urgent business. Lobbyists (representatives of special interest groups or corporations) may intervene, or other senators may introduce competing legislation.

Senator Kenneth Keating of New York (second from right) meets with Jewish lobbyists. Ideas for legislation come from numerous sources, including lobbyists.

The bill's sponsors organize support by enlisting other senators' endorsements and issuing press releases to generate publicity. They tally constituent mail to assess public opinion. They call upon members of their party—and upon like-minded members of the opposition party—to build a coalition supporting the bill. Sometimes, they make concessions and compromises to win other senators' support. They may also employ reciprocity—appealing for votes by promising to vote for other issues in return.

Finally, the committee reports on the bill. The bill dies if the committee disapproves of it. But if the committee reports favorably, it presents the bill to the full Senate for approval. If the bill seems likely to pass, the reporting senator may ask for unanimous consent to the bill. If such consent is granted, the bill is approved without debate or change.

Senators who disapprove of the bill can employ a variety of tactics to delay consent. They may place an informal hold on the bill until the sponsors agree

76

to certain changes. Or they may offer amendments to the bill. These amendments may be germane (specifically related to the bill) or nongermane (unrelated to the bill). Some bills become "Christmas tree" bills—senators hang amendments on them as they would hang ornaments on a Christmas tree. Other overloaded bills are called "cookie jars," because there is something in them for everyone.

On the Senate Floor

If unanimous consent for passage of a bill cannot be obtained, the Senate places the bill on its calendar and the majority leader schedules a debate. The bill's manager—the committee chairman, the subcommittee chairman, or the bill's chief sponsor—makes a speech in its favor. Then the opposition manager states his case. After the managers have spoken, other senators may speak for or against the bill. Unless they have agreed to a time limit, they may speak for as long as they wish. They may state their opinions or offer amendments for the Senate to vote on.

Members of the Senate Republican Policy Committee discuss a bill in 1974. A bill dies if the committee does not approve it, but with the committee's consent, it continues to the full Senate for approval.

A bill's opponents can use many tactics to stop it. They can try to amend its most objectionable features or attempt to make it so unattractive that the full Senate defeats it. And they can demand quorum calls to delay a vote, calling the roll to determine if the necessary minimum number of senators is present. If the bill is extremely controversial, the opposition may launch a filibuster against it, talking indefinitely from the Senate floor to delay the vote. Other bills mount up behind the filibustered bill, pressuring the majority leader to send it back to committee.

The majority leader can employ several tactics against a filibuster. He can adopt a two-track legislative day, devoting part of the day to the filibustered bill and the rest to other legislation. Or he can focus the Senate's entire attention on the filibustered bill, keeping the Senate in session late into the night or even around the clock. This tactic can be dangerous, however. Although it is intended to exhaust the filibustering minority, the majority leader runs the risk of wearing out the majority. Senators called to vote in the middle of the night sometimes lose patience with the best of legislation.

Senators relax on cots during a marathon civil rights debate in 1960. The majority leader can attempt to end a filibuster by prolonging a Senate session indefinitely, thereby exhausting the opposition.

To cut off a filibuster, 13 senators can file a cloture petition. If three-fifths of the senators (60 members) vote for cloture, the filibuster ends. But achieving cloture does not mean the majority has won. Postcloture filibusters, in which opponents load the bill with amendments—sometimes changing just a single word—may be used to delay final passage. However, limits exist on the number of amendments and the amount of time permitted for a postcloture filibuster.

After the debate ends, the Senate votes on the bill. If the bill receives a majority of "nay" votes, it dies. And even if a majority approves the measure, it does not yet become law. The Senate must send all approved measures to the House of Representatives.

A Bill Before the House

After the House receives a Senate bill, it sends the bill to a committee. Like the Senate committee that first reviewed the bill, the House committee may hold hearings to further investigate the bill. It may also attach amendments to it. And, as in the Senate, it then reports on the bill.

If the House committee reports favorably, it places the bill on the calendar and debate begins. If the House fails to pass the bill, it goes back to the Senate and the whole process begins again. If the House and Senate pass different versions of the bill, as they frequently do, then a conference committee, usually composed of members of the committees that originally considered the bill, tries to reach an agreement.

If committee members cannot reach a compromise, the bill dies. However, if the committee makes changes that reconcile the Senate and House bills, it sends a new version of the bill back for another vote. This time, however, both houses must vote on the bill "up or down"—that is, without further amendments. Again, a majority of "nay" votes kills the bill; a majority of "ayes" approves it.

Final Steps

If the House and Senate both approve the bill, one step remains before it becomes law: The president of the United States must sign it. The president usually has three choices: He can sign the bill into law, allow it to become law without his signature by not acting on it within ten days, or veto it. If Congress adjourns or is about to adjourn, the president can refuse to sign the bill for ten

Supreme Court justices pose for a formal portrait following the Senate's confirmation of Chief Justice William Rehnquist (seated, center) in 1986.

days, after which it dies. This maneuver is called a "pocket veto," suggesting that the president places the bill in his pocket without signing it.

If the president signs the bill, it becomes law. But if the president vetoes the bill, he must send Congress an explanatory message. If many senators and congressmen still support the bill, congressional leaders can challenge the president by scheduling a vote to override the veto. A two-thirds majority of both houses is required to override a presidential veto. If the veto is blocked, the bill becomes law.

Administering the Bill

Once a law has been passed, Congress must fund it through an appropriations bill. After the law has been funded, it must be administered by a government agency. The committee that handled the initial legislation usually oversees the administering agency. The committee may periodically hold hearings on the agency's effectiveness in administering the law. It may call witnesses to testify as to the law's value and may recommend additional legislation.

The courts also have the authority to review and interpret new laws. Citizens or groups who object to some aspect of the law can bring a suit against it. This forces the courts to review the law and determine if any portion violates the Constitution or requires judicial interpretation. The case may go as high as the Supreme Court, which can declare acts of Congress unconstitutional. If that court rules against a bill that many congressmen still support, the legislative process begins over again. Congress must enact a version of the bill that satisfies the court's objections.

Passing a law remains an intricate task. Its very complexity guarantees that legislation will reflect long, hard deliberation. The process ensures that the nation's laws will, as much as possible, reflect the concerns and desires of the American people.

In the modern Senate chamber, senators still operate under the Constitutional guidelines established two centuries ago.

SEVEN

Two Centuries of Tradition

Modern visitors to Capitol Hill find a traditional yet dynamic Senate. After two centuries, the Senate still operates under the Constitution's guidelines. But it exercises its own judgment in applying its Constitutional powers. In times of crisis, such as the Civil War and the Great Depression, the Senate has initiated bold legislative reform. At other times, as during the McCarthy era, it has blocked reform.

Throughout its history, the Senate has sometimes led public opinion and sometimes lagged behind. Legislation has lingered in committee for years and then suddenly burst forth in a torrent of debate and enactment. Some presidents, such as Franklin D. Roosevelt, have overwhelmed the Senate and diminished its power. Others, such as Richard M. Nixon, have faced extreme frustration at the Senate's hands.

Whereas the powers of many countries' upper houses have declined, the Senate remains a powerful upper body. It has sole authority to advise on and consent to treaties and nominations and shares power with the House of Representatives to pass legislation. Many modern senators are nationally recognized as authorities on governmental issues. And senators frequently emerge as presidential contenders.

Democratic senator Carl Hayden of Arizona used to advise freshman

Senator Mike Mansfield chats with Senator Edward Brooke, who became the United States' first black senator in 85 years when he was elected in 1966.

senators that there were two kinds of senators: show horses and work horses. "If you want to get your name in the papers, be a show horse," he said. Hayden, who served longer than any other senator, rarely gave a speech and seldom saw his name in the newspapers. Yet he was elected president pro tem, chaired important committees, sponsored major legislation, and gained enormous respect from his colleagues. For many years he epitomized the Senate ideal—a senator whose seniority allowed him to chair important committees and whose collegiality demonstrated respect for the Senate as an institution.

This respect for the Senate continues to transcend party differences. Senators who oppose each other in public frequently socialize with each other, and conservatives and liberals work together to win projects for their states or regions. The Senate builds such strong ties that senators have been reluctant to discipline errant colleagues.

Membership in the Senate remains fairly exclusive. Only 16 women and even fewer black, Hispanic, and Asian Americans have ever served as senators. But in recent years, the number of minority candidates for Senate seats has increased. Television campaigning has allowed candidates to win election without the backing of traditional political connections. Astronauts, athletes, college professors, movie stars, and merchants—some of whom had never before run for office—have taken seats in the chamber.

GLOSSARY

Cloture   A movement to end a filibuster. Three-fifths of the Senate must approve a cloture in order for it to take effect.

Coalition   A temporary alliance of different interest groups or party affiliations in order to enact specific legislation.

Filibuster   A non-stop speech designed to delay enactment of legislation.

Impeachment   An action of Congress charging the president, vice-president, or other civil official with treason, bribery, or other high crimes. The House of Representatives makes the charge and the Senate conducts the trial to hear the impeachment case.

Lobbyists   Representatives of special interest groups or corporations who attempt to influence legislators in their votes.

Omnibus bill   A package of legislation that includes a variety of different proposals.

Partisan committees   Committees established by each party to prepare programs, publish policy papers, and keep voting records.

Party cloakroom   A room near the Senate chamber where party members can meet to discuss party business.

President pro tempore   A senator elected by his or her peers to preside when the president of the Senate is absent.

Quorum   The minimum number of members required to transact legislative business. In the Senate, 51 members constitute a quorum.

Roll-call vote   A vote in which all senators participate by answering "aye" or "nay" when their names are called.

Standing committee A permanent committee established at the beginning of a Congressional term to consider legislative issues within a certain subject area.

Unanimous consent agreement A vote to approve a bill without putting it on the Senate calendar, so that the bill is accepted from the reporting committee without debate or amendment.

Veto The power to prohibit legislation from becoming law.

Whips Party members elected by the Senate who assist the party leader by organizing legislative business.

SELECTED REFERENCES

Baker, Ross K. *Friend and Foe in the U.S. Senate.* New York: Freed Press, 1980.

Congressional Quarterly. Guide to the Congress of the United States; Origins, History, and Procedure. Washington, D.C.: Congressional Quarterly Service, 1982.

Cotton, Norris. *In the Senate, Amidst the Conflict and the Turmoil.* New York: Dodd, Mead & Company, 1978.

Foley, Michael. *The New Senate: Liberal Influence on a Conservative Institution, 1959–1972.* New Haven: Yale University Press, 1980.

Josephy, Alvin M., Jr. *On the Hill: A History of the American Congress.* New York: Simon & Schuster, 1979.

Redman, Eric. *The Dance of Legislation.* New York: Simon & Schuster, 1973.

Reid, T. R. *Congressional Odyssey: The Story of a Senate Bill.* San Francisco: W. H. Freeman & Company, 1980.

Senate Historical Office. *The United States Senate: A Historical Bibliography.* Washington, D.C.: Government Printing Office, 1977.

INDEX

Donald A. Ritchie is the associate historian for the United States Senate. His publications include *Heritage of Freedom: History of the United States* and *James M. Landis: Dean of the Regulators.* He holds a Ph.D. from the University of Maryland and has been a lecturer at the University of Maryland and at George Mason University.

Arthur M. Schlesinger, jr., served in the White House as special assistant to Presidents Kennedy and Johnson. He is the author of numerous acclaimed works in American history and has twice been awarded the Pulitzer Prize. He taught history at Harvard College for many years and is currently Albert Schweitzer Professor of the Humanities at the City College of New York.

The Capitol is located between Constitution and Independence Avenues at First Street in Washington, D.C. It is open to the public daily from 9:00 A.M. to 4:00 P.M., and is closed on Thanksgiving, Christmas, and New Year's Day. Free tours leave every 10 minutes from 9:00 A.M. to 3:45 P.M. in the Rotunda, and include both the Senate and House wings.
